This book belongs to:

....

My First Holy Communion

A storybook for parents and grandparents to help
them prepare their child for First Holy Communion

By Deirdre Mary Ascough | Illustrated by Lisa E Brown

Ignatius · MAGNIFICAT®

To God, who has blessed me with the gifts of life and love.

For my father, *Grandad Matthew*— may the kingdom of heaven be yours.

For my beautiful little girl, Isabelle— and all the other First Holy Communion children—may your special friendship with Jesus be a lifelong and joyful one.

Thank you, Damian, for your constant encouragement and support. You are a true gift to me. And thank you to my dear mother, Carmel, for encouraging us to become saints.

Nihil Obstat: Rev Dr D Vincent Twomey svd, 7 May 2010
Imprimi Potest: ✠ Philip, Bishop of Raphoe, 12 May 2010

First published in Falcarragh, Co. Donegal, Ireland by Clonmacnois Press in 2010 | *www.clonmacnoispress.com*
Second edition printed in 2011
Third edition printed in 2012
© 2010 Deirdre Mary Ascough & Clonmacnois Press
Design by Paula Nolan & Áine Kierans

Printed by TWP, Singapore
Printed on August 5, 2013
Job Number MGN 13009
Printed in compliance with the Consumer Protection Safety Act of 2008

Contents

CHAPTER ONE

God and the Beginning

efore there was anything—any tree, any flower, any earth and sky, any person— there was God. God Who always was and forever will be. God Who is beautiful, Who is truthful, Who is very good and, especially, Who is love.

God is three persons in one: the Father, the Son and the Holy Spirit, Who love one another very much. We call this the Trinity. Long ago Saint Patrick used a little shamrock leaf (with its three parts) to explain the three persons of the Trinity.

There are three persons in one God.
Each of the persons is God.

There are not three gods, but only one God.

God is so wonderful and amazing that we can never fully understand—or even imagine—what He is like! Even though God is far greater than we are, He has shown us and told us a lot about Himself so that we can come to know Him and to love Him. (We will especially see this later when we read about what Jesus taught us.)

In the beginning, God created the whole universe. It is so amazing that many scientists spend their whole lives trying to find out how God did it. Like a master artist, He made so many beautiful things that we can see.

All the designers in the world could never have designed anything as wonderful and as detailed, and yet so simple, as God's creation—from the little seahorse in the great ocean to the wild horse on the prairies. From the little starfish on the beach to the twinkling star in the night sky. There was beauty, harmony, pattern and meaning in all things. And it was all good.

And God continues to keep all these things going!

CHAPTER THREE

God's Wonderful Plan

And so God had a plan. The Bible tells us the great story of His master plan. There are two parts of the Bible. The Old Testament is the part of the Bible where we read about the many ways God spoke with people in order to lead them back to Himself so that, when the time was right, He could give us the greatest gift of all—Jesus—the promised Savior. Jesus is the way back to the Father, and to the Father's house. We read all about Jesus in the New Testament part of the Bible.

In the Old Testament there was Noah and there was Abraham; there was Moses and then David; then there was Isaiah.

Noah was a man who loved God at a time when everyone else didn't care about Him. All the people were doing wicked things. God asked Noah to build a great big boat and to take his family and two of every animal into it because He was going to send a flood to destroy everything upon the earth.

Noah did as God had asked, and Noah, his family and the animals were safe. After the flood, God promised He would not destroy the earth with water again. He made a rainbow in the sky as a sign of His promise.

Some time later there was a man named Abraham, who also loved God very much. God called him to be the father of a great people—God's Chosen People. But Abraham and his wife, Sarah, had no children. One day God promised to give them a child and a portion of land. He told Abraham that he would have many descendants. For a long time no child came. God was testing Abraham's faith, and Abraham continued to trust God and to believe in His promises. Then a baby boy was born to Abraham and Sarah, and they called him Isaac. When Isaac was a boy, God tested Abraham again by asking him to give up his son. Abraham's heart was very heavy as he prepared to give his son back to God. But God sent an angel to stop Abraham when He saw Abraham's faithfulness and obedience to Him. Just as Abraham offered his son Isaac, God the Father gave up His only Son, Jesus, for us. As God had promised, Abraham's descendants grew numerous. They were the Chosen People, which now includes all who have faith like Abraham.

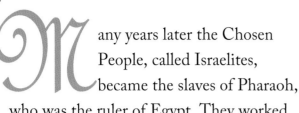

Many years later the Chosen People, called Israelites, became the slaves of Pharaoh, who was the ruler of Egypt. They worked hard and were treated badly. They cried out to God to help them and to set them free. God sent Moses to lead His people out of Egypt. Moses asked Pharaoh to release God's people, but he refused. So God told His people to gather in their homes for the Passover. They ate a meal of roasted lamb and unleavened bread. They marked their outer doors with the blood of the lamb so that the angel of death would pass over them as it struck down the firstborn of the Egyptians. God's people were saved by the blood of the lamb. Pharaoh was afraid and let them go. The Israelites followed Moses out of Egypt and wandered for forty years in the desert before they entered the land God had promised to Abraham. God provided for all of their needs, and He gave Moses laws to govern His people. God asked them to show their love and faithfulness by making sacrifices to Him. He blessed them for their obedience, and He promised to take away their sins. But these sacrifices would one day be replaced by the greatest one of all.

During their time in the desert, God gave the Ten Commandments to Moses on the top of Mount Sinai. They were carved on stone and were kept in a special container called the Ark of the Covenant. God made a promise to be faithful to His people (to love them and to stay with them always), and they promised to be faithful to Him (to love Him as their only God and to love others). This is called a covenant.

Some time later a young boy named David saved his people from their enemies the Philistines. There was a giant named Goliath in the Philistine army, and if the Israelites could not beat him in single combat, they would become slaves of the Philistine king. David was a shepherd boy and was accustomed to defending his sheep from dangerous wild animals with his sling. He defeated Goliath by knocking him down with a stone from his sling. The Israelites won the war, and later David became their king.

David loved God and served his people well. God promised him that his throne would stand firm forever and that the Messiah would come from his descendants. The Messiah, or Savior, would be the bridge between God and us. He would free us from the slavery of sin and reunite us with God. Mary and Joseph came from the family line of King David, and Jesus, Mary's son, did too!

Often in the Old Testament times, God sent prophets to remind His people to love and to serve Him. The prophets also foretold what would happen and spoke often about the promised One, the Messiah, Who would free the Chosen People once and for all. One of the prophets, Isaiah, described the Messiah in these words (and the description sounds just like Jesus):
Like a lamb . . . he was silent and opened not his mouth . . . he had done no wrong nor spoken any falsehood . . . he shall take away the sins of many, and win pardon for their offenses. (Isaiah 53:7,9,12)

Another prophet also wrote about the Savior:
They have pierced my hands and feet; I can count all my bones. (Psalm 22:17-18)

And so the Chosen People awaited the coming of the Savior.

CHAPTER FOUR

God Sends His Son

When the time was right, God the Father chose a Jewish girl named Mary to be the mother of His beloved Son. God prepared her even before she was born by creating her pure, free from original sin and full of love.

Mary was betrothed[1] to Joseph when God sent His messenger, the archangel Gabriel, to ask her if she would be the mother of Jesus. She said yes to God, and through the power of the Holy Spirit baby Jesus grew within her.

I am the handmaid of the Lord.

Luke 1:38

An angel came to Joseph in a dream and told him that God was the father of Mary's baby. Mary and Joseph married, and Joseph became the foster father of Jesus. When baby Jesus was born, the angels brought the shepherds to worship Him. A great star brought the three wise kings to adore Him. Although He was God, He came to us as a simple little baby, born into a poor family. God makes Himself small for us. He places Himself in our arms. The Father comes to us in His Son Jesus. He asks for our love! God lives with us!

John 3:16

For God so loved the world that he gave his only Son.

As a little child Jesus learned to be obedient to His mother and father. He helped with the work at home and in the workshop. As He grew up in His home town of Nazareth, Jesus was kind and good to the people around Him and many liked Him very much. Jesus went often to the synagogue with His parents and the other families. There He learned the Ten Commandments, and listened to the stories about Noah, Abraham, Moses, King David and many others. His parents and teachers taught Him about God and His great love for His people. Jesus loved His Father in heaven very much.

When He was twelve years old He went with His parents on a pilgrimage to the city of Jerusalem. When they were returning home, Jesus got lost in the great crowds of people, and His parents spent three days looking for Him. But where was He? He was in the Temple (which was like a big church) speaking to the teachers of the Jewish faith, who were amazed at His wisdom. He was so young and yet He understood so much about God. When Mary and Joseph found Him there He said to them, "Why were you looking for me? Did you not know that I must be in my Father's house?" (Luke 2:49). He went home with His parents and continued each day to love God and the people around Him.

CHAPTER FIVE

Jesus' Mission

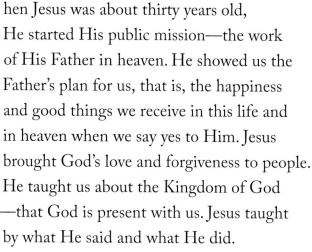

hen Jesus was about thirty years old, He started His public mission—the work of His Father in heaven. He showed us the Father's plan for us, that is, the happiness and good things we receive in this life and in heaven when we say yes to Him. Jesus brought God's love and forgiveness to people. He taught us about the Kingdom of God —that God is present with us. Jesus taught by what He said and what He did.

Jesus told many stories called parables to teach the people about the Kingdom of God. Each of these stories had a message, for example, the parable of the Prodigal Son teaches us about God's love and forgiveness, no matter what we do:

There was once a father with two sons. One day the younger son asked his father for a large amount of his fortune. The father granted his son's request. Off went the young man to a faraway land, where he spent the money foolishly. After some time, his money was all spent and he went looking for work. He found a job taking care of pigs and was so hungry that he sometimes ate the pigs' food.

Then he decided to return to his father's house and ask him for a better job. His father saw him coming from a long way off and ran to greet his younger son. The young man apologized and asked his father to forgive him. His father had a big welcome home party for his long lost son, who had returned. In his great love for his son, he forgave him and opened his heart and his home to him again. (from Luke 15:11-32)

Jesus told the parable of the Good Samaritan in order to teach us about the importance of loving the other people around us and of not judging them wrongly:

There was once a Jewish man who went on a long journey. On his way he was attacked and robbed by thieves, who then left him to die at the side of the road. Some people who saw him there just passed him by and did not help him. They rushed on, too busy to help or frightened that they too might be attacked if they delayed. Then a man from a region called Samaria came along—the Jews did not like the Samaritans—and stopped to help the injured man. He bandaged the sick man's wounds and, putting him on his donkey, brought him to a nearby inn. There he gave the innkeeper money to feed and care for the sick man until he was well again. (from Luke 10:30-37)

Jesus performed many miracles to show us that the Kingdom of God is near. He did these miracles because He wanted to do good things for us and to help us believe that God loves us. Jesus freed many people from the power of evil spirits. He healed many who were sick and forgave sins.

At a wedding party, He turned six large jars of water into wine because the bride and groom had no more wine left to serve their guests. He fed over five thousand hungry people by multiplying two small fish and five loaves of bread into enough food for them all.

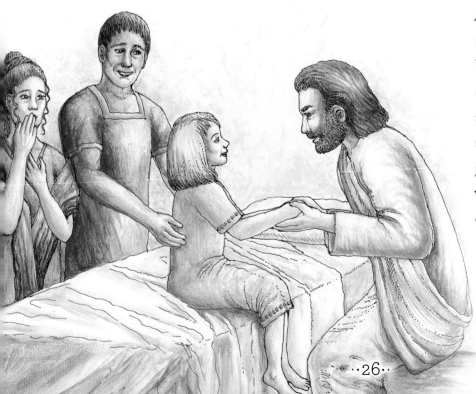

Another time Jesus brought a little girl back to life. She had been very sick and when Jesus came to her house, she had already died. He took her hand and told her, "Come my little girl", and she sat up and was well again. That was the miracle of Jairus' daughter.

He walked on the water and calmed the big storm on the Sea of Galilee. There were many more miracles that He did so that we would believe Him and know that He is God.

But the greatest thing Jesus did was to give His life for us. Many wicked people had come to hate Jesus and plotted to have Him killed. They were uncomfortable with His teaching and refused to believe that Jesus was the Messiah. Their hard hearts were closed to His message of love and forgiveness. After three years of teaching and serving His people, Jesus knew that His enemies were closing in on Him and planning to have Him executed. He knew also that His time had come to give Himself up to the Father as a sacrifice for us. On the night before He died, He celebrated the Passover meal with His Apostles. This was the Last Supper.

That night Jesus was arrested. The next day He was cruelly whipped and mocked. He never fought back or spoke in anger to the people who were hurting Him. When He was weak and tired, He was made to carry a heavy cross. He was carrying the sins of everyone—including ours. He was nailed to this cross, and even as He was dying He asked God to forgive His killers. As on the first Passover, here was a sacrificial lamb whose blood saved the people from death and won their freedom. Behold, Jesus is the Lamb of God, Who takes away the sins of the world!

During the next forty days Jesus appeared to His Apostles to prepare them to lead the Church in its mission. Then He ascended into heaven. Ten days later He sent them the Holy Spirit. This great event occurred on the Jewish feast of Pentecost, which celebrates the giving of the Ten Commandments. The Holy Spirit brought courage and joy to the followers of Jesus—and so the Church was born. The Holy Spirit has always been with us ever since!

Jesus said too that He would be with His Church always. And He said He is coming back, but we don't know when!

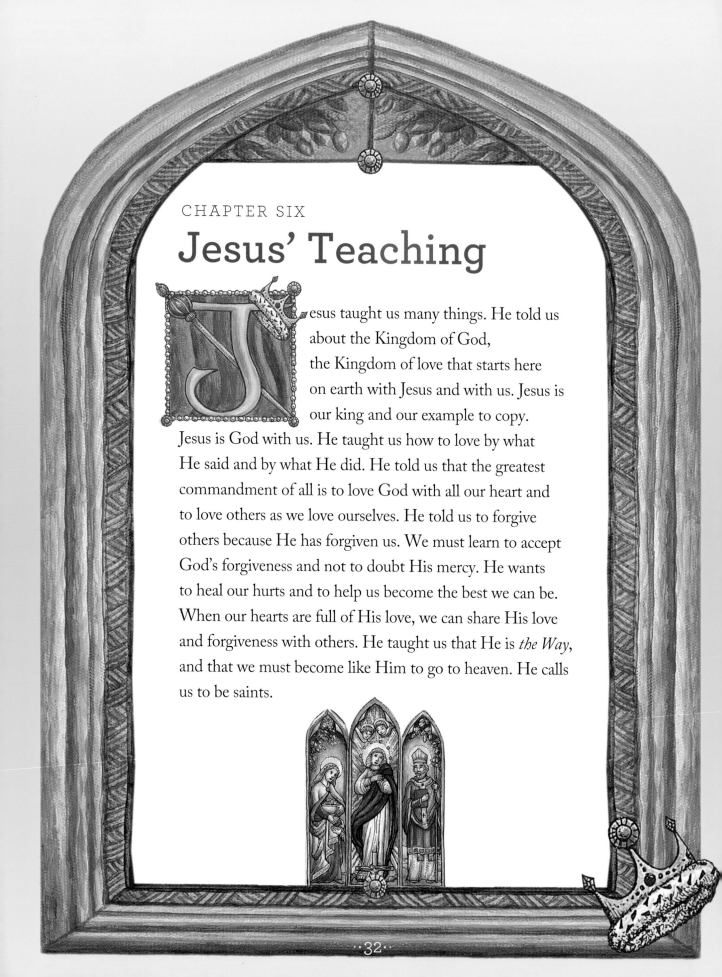

CHAPTER SIX

Jesus' Teaching

Jesus taught us many things. He told us about the Kingdom of God, the Kingdom of love that starts here on earth with Jesus and with us. Jesus is our king and our example to copy. Jesus is God with us. He taught us how to love by what He said and by what He did. He told us that the greatest commandment of all is to love God with all our heart and to love others as we love ourselves. He told us to forgive others because He has forgiven us. We must learn to accept God's forgiveness and not to doubt His mercy. He wants to heal our hurts and to help us become the best we can be. When our hearts are full of His love, we can share His love and forgiveness with others. He taught us that He is *the Way*, and that we must become like Him to go to heaven. He calls us to be saints.

One day a little boy went with his mother to visit a nearby church. It was a bright, sunny day, and the sunlight shone through the stained-glass windows. There were many pictures of different people in the colored glass of the windows. The boy pointed to the images and asked, "Who are those people in the windows?"

"They are the saints in heaven", replied his mother. After some time in quiet thought, the little boy said aloud, "Oh, the saints, they must be the people who let the light shine through them".

We too can become saints when we let the light of Jesus shine through us. Jesus asks us to be like Him, to be kind and brave. He asks us to be His hands and feet, to be His smile and voice in our world, in our family and with the people we meet.

One day Jesus went up a hill and sat down with the many people who had gathered to listen to Him. He taught them the Beatitudes. These are the good ways that we can behave toward God and other people. Jesus asks us to live the Beatitudes each day. He promises us that this is the way to real happiness and joy. He asks us to be prayerful, to be caring, to be gentle, to be fair, to be forgiving, to be respectful, to be a peacemaker and to be brave.

But it is hard to love, to give, to forgive, to live as Jesus says. We try but we often fail. We tend to become lazy and to think only of ourselves. But Jesus tells us, "For God all things are possible" (Matthew 19:26). Jesus helps us, walks with us and forgives us when we fail. He sends us the Holy Spirit to help us and gives us the sacraments to strengthen us.

Do to others as I have done to you,
Speak in kindness only what is true.
Give your gifts of help, love and care,
Not selfishly giving only what is spare.
Be holy like I am holy, for it is the best way
To be happy and free and go to heaven one day.
Pray for those who are mean and bad,
Who hurt you and make Me sad.
I, Jesus, died for each of those too:
I love them and I truly love you.

Why should we say yes to Jesus and do what He tells us?

Because God the Father wants us to be holy and happy on earth and in heaven with Him.

Because of Jesus' love for us and what He has done for us. It is our way of saying, "Thank you, Jesus!" It is our way of saying, "I love you Jesus!"

And because that's the only way we will be truly happy and make other people around us happy.

"Do not be afraid", Jesus told us. "Open wide the door of your hearts to Me and let Me come in." Jesus respects us and our freedom to say yes or no to Him. He will not take anything from us, least of all our freedom. Instead He asks us to use our freedom to become the person God wants us to be, with all our gifts and talents.

Long ago, Saint Ireneus said, "The glory of God is the human person fully alive." This means that God is glorified when we become all He intends us to be, when He writes the beautiful story of our life! Even when our life doesn't seem so beautiful because we are having a very hard time—no matter what, God can make it beautiful because He can turn sorrow into joy. He is our friend, Who walks with us and leads us to our home in heaven with Him.

Jesus gave us His Church, the Church He loved and made holy, so that He could be always with us to guide us and to help us.

CHAPTER SEVEN

The Church

 he Church[2] is God's family. When we are baptized Jesus brings us into this family. It is a very big family! The Church includes all the people who have gone before us who were faithful to Jesus and are happy in heaven now. Think of all the saints whose names we know and the many others we don't know! And there are all the people who have gone before us who are not yet ready to go to heaven. They must spend some time in the waiting place of purgatory. It is a time of purification, of being made ready to meet God face to face in their heavenly home. Perhaps for them purgatory is like being on a long, hot journey through a desert, knowing that they will arrive one day at their Father's house. We can pray for them there so that they can soon be with our heavenly Father.

The Church also includes the people alive today, and living all over the world, who are faithful to Jesus and are on their pilgrimage journey to heaven. All of us in the Church are the Communion of Saints, and we all pray together to our God, and for each other.

Throughout the Old Testament, God had made a covenant with His Chosen People, Israel, promising to be always with them and to care for them. God has made a New Covenant, this time with all peoples. Jesus is the New Covenant—God's binding promise of love and faithfulness with all peoples of all times through Jesus. God gathers together a new people; the Church is this People of God scattered throughout the world. Through the Catholic Church, God calls the entire human race to Himself.

The Church serves and works for both God and all mankind. God wants everybody to come home to heaven, but He Who has created us and has given us free will does not force us. We come to our home in heaven freely, through Jesus and His Church. The Catholic Church is the Church that Jesus started while He was still here on earth. She continues Jesus' saving work of bringing all peoples home to the Father.

Before He returned to the Father's house, Jesus gave us the Apostles as the leaders of the Church. He gave them His power. He gave them His work of forgiving, healing and teaching. He asked them to be ready to lay down their lives for their people as He did Himself. And many died following His example. The Pope, the bishops and the priests continue the work of the Apostles.

With the help of the Holy Spirit, they lead us on the way of holiness to heaven. Jesus made Peter the head of the Apostles. The Pope is the successor of Peter, and the Holy Spirit helps him to guide the whole Church.

Through the Church Jesus gives us the gift of the sacraments. Jesus wants to meet us in the sacraments. He wants to talk to us; He wants to walk with us today, just as He did when He was living on earth many years ago. This He can do because He is the Risen Lord.

He wants to be close to us and to share everything with us—our happy times, our sad times, our problems, our successes and our failures—everything! And it is in the sacraments that we can be especially close to Him.

There are seven sacraments: Baptism, Confession, Eucharist, Confirmation, Marriage, Holy Orders and Anointing of the Sick. A sacrament is a visible sign of an invisible reality—God's gift of Himself. God uses ordinary things to do extraordinary things.

For example, when the priest prays the prayers of Consecration at Mass, the Holy Spirit comes upon the bread and wine, and they become really and truly the Body, Blood, Soul and Divinity of Jesus. It is a wonder each time.

Confirmation

Eucharist

Holy Orders

Confession

Marriage

Anointing of the Sick

Through Baptism we are reborn as children of God and so become members of God's family. When we were baptized as a baby, the priest poured the water over our head saying, "I baptize you . . . *(your Christian name)* in the name of the Father and of the Son and of the Holy Spirit." In Baptism we receive the new life that Jesus won for us in His dying and rising.

This new life is God's life in our hearts. We are reborn as children of God and are now forever His sons and daughters. Baptism takes away the original sin that we are born with.

Long ago, Saint Teresa said that our hearts are a castle where the King lives. God is His Majesty within us! We have been made holy by Baptism, which places the life of God within us. This is why we are to be saints. Baptism is one of the three sacraments that puts a special seal or mark on our soul. It changes us forever.

♪*Joy is the flag flown high over the castle of my heart because the King is in residence there.*♪

Baptism

CHAPTER EIGHT

Confession

The sacrament of Reconciliation, or Confession, wipes away the sins we commit after our Baptism. Our souls are made clean again, and God's life, or grace, is put back into our hearts. When we are sorry for our sins and confess them, we meet Jesus and receive from Him the forgiveness of the Father. We are healed from the hurt that sin does to us.

Sin is doing things that are bad for us, and it makes us sad and lonely. When we sin we stop living in the life of God and start becoming less loving, less good and less beautiful. Some sins are worse than others. Smaller sins are called venial sins, and bigger sins are called mortal sins.[3]

When God made each one of us, He gave us a conscience. Deep within us we know that we should do good things and not bad things. To help our conscience know more clearly what is right and wrong, God gave us the Ten Commandments. The first three tell us about how to love and to respect God. The others tell us about how to love and to respect other people. Most of all, He gave us Jesus to show us how to live and how to love God, ourselves and the people around us—especially in our family.

Before going to Confession we sit or kneel quietly and open our hearts to God, asking Him to help us to know our sins. As we think about what is right and wrong, and the way Jesus wants us to live, we remember the times when we did not act as we should. This is called an examination of conscience *(see pages 66 and 67).*

We ask Jesus to help us to be really and truly sorry for our sins. With all our hearts we will try not to sin again. We know that we will try hard each day to live as Jesus wants. When we are tempted, it helps to ask, "Jesus, what would you do now?" or to say, "Please help me, Jesus!"

In Confession we meet Jesus. He meets us through the priest. We tell our sins to the priest, and he might talk to us a little. He gives us a penance, which is often some prayers. We say we're sorry for our sins because we realize that they have hurt Jesus, Who loves us.

The priest forgives us in the name of God.[4] Our sins are absolved. They are wiped away and gone forever! With joy in our hearts, we thank God for His great love for us, and we pray our penance prayers. Later, we try, if possible, to do something to fix the damage that our sin has done. For example, if I stole my little sister's piggy bank, I should give it, and anything I took out of it, back to her and say I am sorry. If I teased my younger brother and made him cry, I should say sorry to him. After our First Confession we are ready to receive Jesus into our hearts at our First Holy Communion!

*Bless me, Father, for I have sinned. This is
my First Confession, and these are my sins . . .*
[Tell the priest your sins]
For these and all my sins I am very sorry.

ACT OF SORROW

*O my God, I am heartily sorry for all my
sins because they offend You, my God,
Who are totally good and deserve all
my love. I firmly resolve with the help of
Your grace to sin no more and to avoid
whatever leads me to sin. Amen.*

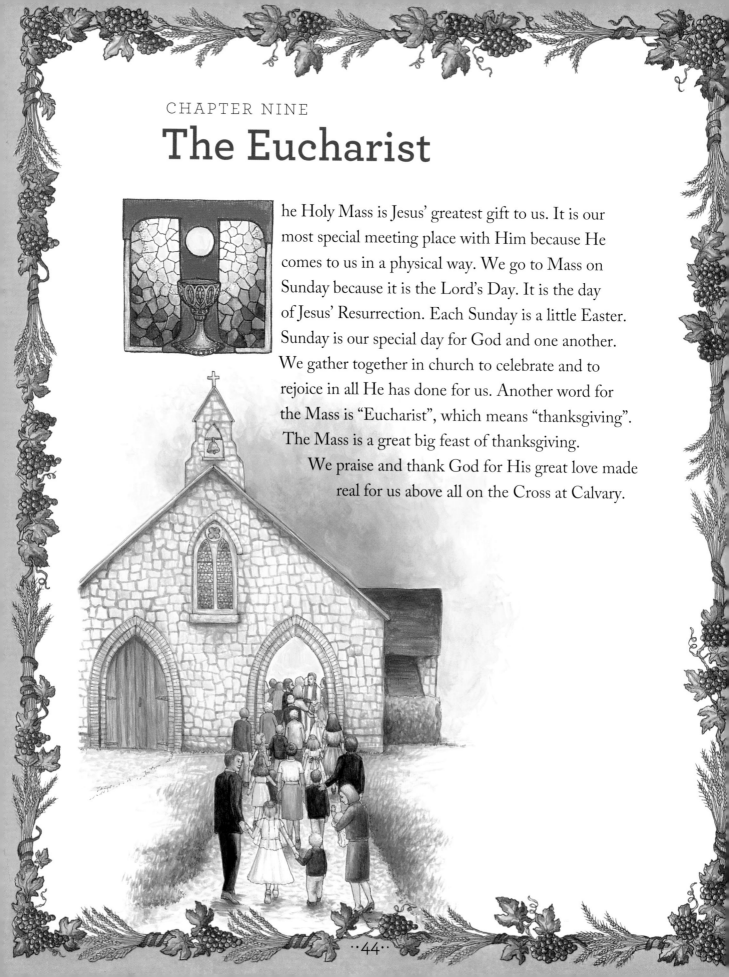

CHAPTER NINE

The Eucharist

he Holy Mass is Jesus' greatest gift to us. It is our most special meeting place with Him because He comes to us in a physical way. We go to Mass on Sunday because it is the Lord's Day. It is the day of Jesus' Resurrection. Each Sunday is a little Easter. Sunday is our special day for God and one another. We gather together in church to celebrate and to rejoice in all He has done for us. Another word for the Mass is "Eucharist", which means "thanksgiving". The Mass is a great big feast of thanksgiving.

We praise and thank God for His great love made real for us above all on the Cross at Calvary.

Jesus gave us the Sacrament of the Eucharist at the Last Supper, at the cross on Calvary, and at His Resurrection. At Mass we come into the presence of God and join our lives with Him. We receive the blessings and good things that God has for us. We see that God walks with us in our life through the bad times and the happy times.

His arms are around us in everything we do—at home, at school, when we play with our friends, when we are sick. We tell God we are sorry for our sins, and we ask His help to be better. He teaches us through the readings and the preaching of the priest, which helps us to know what to do and how to think as we live each day.

Something very wonderful happens at the part of the Mass called the Consecration. The priest calls the Holy Spirit to come down upon the bread and wine so that they can become the Body and Blood of Jesus. These are the words he prays:

What were once bread and wine have become really and truly the Body, Blood, Soul and Divinity of Jesus. There is a big word for this change— "transubstantiation". What looks like bread and wine is now Jesus really present with us. We call this His Real Presence.[5]

Take this, all of you, and eat of it, for this is My Body which will be given up for you . . . (over the bread).

Take this, all of you, and drink from it, for this is the chalice of My Blood, the Blood of the new and eternal covenant, which will be poured out for you and for many for the forgiveness of sins. Do this in memory of Me . . . (over the wine).

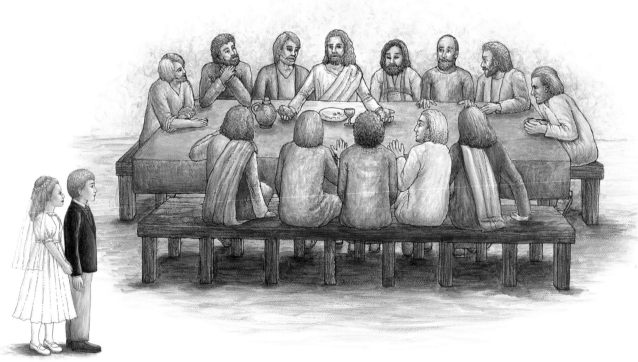

We are now present with Jesus as He gathers with His loved ones at the Last Supper; we are present with Him as He carries His Cross; we are present with Him at the Cross as He lays down His life for us; we are present with Him at His rising from the dead on Easter Sunday. And He is totally present with us in His Body and Blood, in His Soul and Divinity. Being at Mass is almost like a sort of time travel!

We are with Jesus, and we offer ourselves, as well as our loved ones, our joys, sadness, questions and prayers to the Father in heaven through the Holy Spirit. Heaven and earth come together in this wonderful celebration. The angels too give all their love to Jesus and worship at the altar. The Church, the family of God, prays with the Holy Spirit for each member of the family and all the peoples of the world.

Jesus celebrates the Passover and gives us the gift of the Eucharist *(freedom from slavery & death through the blood of the lamb)*.

Jesus offers Himself up for us.

What looks like bread and wine is truly Jesus Himself (transubstantiation).

Heaven and earth . . . .

JESUS THE

No one has greater love than this, to lay down one's life for one's friends.
(John 15:13)

Jesus is risen from the dead *(Jesus gives us new life).*

...are joined together

For ourselves and others we pray for help, healing, forgiveness, strength, peace, freedom, counsel and joy.

We offer all that we have —our lives, joys, sadness, talents— and all that we are to God.

INNOCENT LAMB

We are gathered around the table of the Lord. As I prepare myself to receive Jesus I say, "I am sorry, Jesus, for the times I have said or done something wrong and hurt You. Dear Jesus, please make my heart a nice place for You to come and to live. Please make me holy. I want to be like You. I love You, Jesus".

Right before Communion we pray, "Lord, I am not worthy that You should enter under my roof, but only say the word and my soul shall be healed." Jesus heals our hurts and makes our hearts ready for God. We receive Holy Communion with respect and then kneel quietly for a little while and talk with Jesus. Jesus is in our body and our soul in a very special way. We are very close to Him. Jesus can help us when we ask Him to, and this is a good time to ask Him. He gives us courage. He gives us freedom and makes us happy.

As we leave Mass we are filled with God's power and strength, and so we can love God and one another.

Jesus said, "Whoever eats my flesh and drinks my blood has eternal life...[he] remains in me and I in him." (John 6:54,56)

THE BREAD OF LIFE

Now God's life and love is in my soul,
Freeing me, healing me and making me whole!
It makes me grow as God's child,
He holds me, He hugs me, I am no longer exiled!
It makes me strong and healthy too,
Helping me, showing me the right thing to do!

Our First Holy Communion day is a very special day, and we dress in our special clothes. But what is more important than the clothes is how we feel on the inside. We are happy and ready to receive Jesus! And there will be many other days that we will receive Jesus in Holy Communion again.

The Miracle of Lanciano

A long time ago, in a small town in Italy called Lanciano, there was a doubting priest. He doubted many things about the faith, but he especially doubted that the bread and wine consecrated on the altar could turn into the Real Presence of Jesus. "How could God—Who is greater than the universe—come to us disguised as simple bread and wine?" he asked himself.

One day as he celebrated Mass in his little church, an extraordinary thing happened. When he said the words of Consecration he saw the appearances of the bread and wine change into that of human flesh and blood. The priest was amazed and filled with wonder. He thanked and praised God as he realized that the wonder of the Eucharist that he saw that day was the same wonder that happened invisibly at every Holy Mass in every time and in every place. And he doubted no more![6]

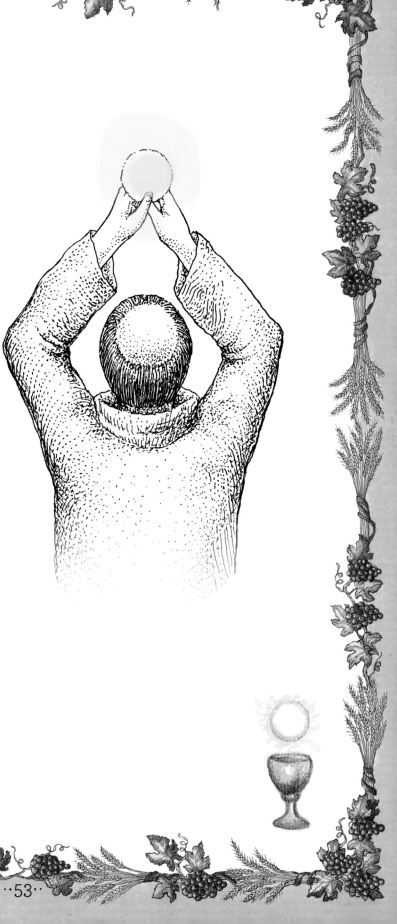

CHAPTER TEN

Parts of the Mass

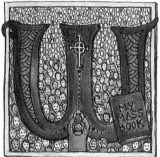 hen we know what is happening during the different parts of the Mass, we can understand something of the great mystery of the Eucharist. Here all of creation, visible and invisible, is worshipping God Who is love. And we can join in too! This is our family celebration! There are four main parts to the Mass.

1 *Introductory Rites*

Entrance

The priest goes to the altar and begins the Mass with the Sign of the Cross *(In the Name of the Father and of the Son and of the Holy Spirit. Amen.)*

Penitential Act

We think of our sins and tell God we are very sorry. We lay them at the foot of the Cross, where Jesus offered up His life for the forgiveness of our sins. We ask for God's mercy as we prepare our hearts, making them shining clean for Jesus to come in Holy Communion!

Gloria

We praise and thank God for His goodness.

2   *Liturgy of the Word*

First Reading

We usually listen to stories from the Old Testament part of the Bible about the People of God as they awaited the coming of the Messiah.

Responsorial Psalm

The Psalms are Old Testament hymns of praise, thanksgiving and calls for help. The psalm becomes our own prayer too as we listen to the verses and pray the response.

Second Reading

We hear from the Acts of the Apostles or the letters in the New Testament, which the Apostles wrote to teach the early Christians, and us, how to live and to love like Jesus.

Alleluia

We sing "Alleluia", which means "praise the Lord."

Gospel

We listen to the life and teaching of Jesus as found in the four Gospels (Matthew, Mark, Luke and John) of the New Testament. We stand for the Gospel as the priest reads it for us.

Homily

The priest teaches us more about the Scripture readings and helps us to see what Jesus is telling us in the story of our own life.

Profession of Faith

We say the Creed, which is what we believe as Catholics about God and what He has done for us.

Intercessory Prayers

We pray for all who need God's help: the Pope, the bishops and priests, our leaders, the sick and suffering, the poor all over the world, our family and friends, ourselves and all those who have died.

3 *Liturgy of the Eucharist*

Offering of Gifts

We give a gift of money to help the Church and the people who are in need in our community. We bring our gifts of bread and wine to the altar.

Eucharistic Prayer

A prayer of praise and thanksgiving to God for all the good things He has done for us and especially for the gift of His Son, Jesus. The high point of the Mass is the Consecration. The priest calls the Holy Spirit down upon the gifts. He prays the same words Jesus said at the Last Supper. At this moment the bread and wine become the Body and Blood of Jesus. Jesus is fully and completely present in His Body and Blood, Soul and Divinity! The priest lifts up the Body and Blood of Jesus so that we can worship Him and love Him! This is the wonder of every Mass! Jesus is present to us in His sacrificial love on the Cross.

Acclamation of Faith

We respond to what God (the Father, the Son and the Holy Spirit) has done and say, "Save us, Savior of the world, for by your Cross and Resurrection you have set us free", or, "We proclaim your Death, O Lord, and profess your Resurrection until you come again."

Our Father

We pray the prayer to our heavenly Father, that Jesus taught us.

Sign of Peace

We offer the peace of Jesus to those around us.

| Holy Communion | We are going to meet someone very wonderful, and so we behave respectfully. We receive the Body and Blood of Jesus and say "Amen" (which means: "yes, I believe"). We must not eat or drink anything (except water or medicine) for one hour before receiving Holy Communion.[7] |

| Prayer After Communion | Jesus is with us in a very special way, and we talk quietly to Him in our hearts. He is our friend, and we enjoy this time together with Him. We listen to what He says to us. This is not a time to look around or to talk with friends. The priest prays a prayer of thanks. |

Concluding (ending) Rites

| Blessing | The priest blesses the people and sends them forth in peace to love and serve the Lord and one another. We have a new strength to love, to be generous and to be kind and helpful to those around us! |

CHAPTER ELEVEN
Other Sacraments

esus meets us and blesses us in the other sacraments too. A few years after our First Holy Communion, we receive the Sacrament of Confirmation. For couples who are getting married, there is the Sacrament of Marriage. When a man becomes a priest, he receives the Sacrament of Holy Orders. And finally the old and the sick can receive the Sacrament of Anointing. God is always with us, but He comes to us at special times in our lives to be with us in a special way and to bless us. The sacraments are these moments. And the great thing is that we can meet Him every week, and indeed every day, in the Sacrament of the Eucharist!

Confirmation is the sacrament of the Holy Spirit. The Holy Spirit comes upon us in a new way, strengthening us in our faith, helping us to live more like Jesus and to tell others the good news of the Father's love and plan for us. In this sacrament too our soul receives the special seal of the gift of the Spirit.

The first miracle that Jesus did was at a wedding in a place called Cana. Jesus and His mother, Mary, were among the invited guests. His presence and His miracle teach us that marriage is holy. The head waiter discovered that there was not enough wine left for the guests. Jesus' mother asked Him to do something to help the newly married couple. He turned six large jars of water into wine so that there was more than enough for everyone!

Just as Jesus changed the water into wine, He changes human love into divine love when married couples are joined together in Him. That means that God helps husbands and wives to love like He loves—with open, generous and forgiving hearts. God also shows us His love through the love of parents. When we are loved by our mother and father, we feel God's love in our hearts.

For Catholics, marriage is a sacrament.

The Sacrament of Holy Orders was given to us by Jesus when He called His Apostles to Himself and then sent them to the ends of the earth to tell of the good news of God's love and plan for us.

When the bishop ordains new priests, they receive power from the Holy Spirit to serve the people of God, to forgive sins in the name of Jesus, to anoint the sick and to offer the holy sacrifice of the Mass.

Although they carry a precious treasure, they are also human and can make mistakes. They are gifts to us from Jesus because if we had no priests we could not have Mass and most of the other sacraments. We can pray for them, that they receive the strength to live like Jesus and to serve Him and His people well. This sacrament also leaves a special seal on the soul that will always remain.[8]

In the Sacrament of the Anointing of the Sick, the priest lays his hands on the head of a very sick person and anoints his hands and forehead with blessed oil. He prays with him so that the Holy Spirit comes upon him. The sins of the sick person are forgiven (if he cannot go to Confession) and he receives a special strength to give himself to Jesus, to be healed, or to endure his illness and suffering.[9]

CHAPTER TWELVE

Prayer

hen God created human persons a long time ago, it was because He loved us. Since then, He has never left His children, and He never will. Each day He is with us when we get up in the morning, when we are at school, when we are with our friends, when we are at home with our family or on holidays. He is with us in all our choices.

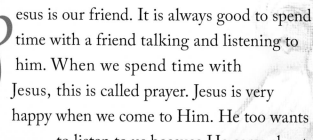

esus is our friend. It is always good to spend time with a friend talking and listening to him. When we spend time with Jesus, this is called prayer. Jesus is very happy when we come to Him. He too wants to listen to us because He cares about all our problems and stories. And we can listen to Him too. He helps us make the right choices. Although we cannot see Him, He is there, just as the wind and air, although we cannot see them, are there.

We can pray to God at any time and in every place. There are many ways to pray. We can just say our own words to Jesus. We can pray to God the Father the way Jesus told us with the Our Father prayer. Or we can pray many other prayers. Our guardian angel always prays with us too.

We can also write our own prayer to Jesus:

Try to write a special prayer for after receiving Jesus in Holy Communion. You can write it like a letter to Him . . .

Dear Jesus,
I am so happy that you are my friend. Thank you
for coming so close to me in Holy Communion.
Please help me to be good and kind. Please bless
me. Please bless my family and friends. Thank you
for all the good things you have given me.
I love you, Jesus.

Signed,

....

When we begin and end our prayers, we make the Sign of the Cross: In the name of the Father and of the Son and of the Holy Spirit. Amen.[10]

Our Father

Our Father, who art in heaven, hallowed be thy name; thy kingdom come, thy will be done on earth as it is in heaven. *Give us this day our daily bread, and forgive us our trespasses, as we forgive those who trespass against us; and lead us not into temptation, but deliver us from evil. Amen.*

Hail Mary

Hail Mary, full of grace. The Lord is with thee. Blessed art thou among women, and blessed is the fruit of thy womb, Jesus. *Holy Mary, Mother of God, pray for us sinners, now and at the hour of our death. Amen.*

Glory Be

Glory be to the Father, and to the Son and to the Holy Spirit. *As it was in the beginning, is now, and ever shall be, world without end. Amen.*

Grace Before Meals

Bless us, O Lord, and these Your gifts, which we are about to receive from Your bounty. Through Christ our Lord. Amen.

Act of Sorrow

O my God, I am heartily sorry for all my sins because they offend You, my God, Who are totally good and deserve all my love. I firmly resolve with the help of Your grace to sin no more and to avoid whatever leads me to sin. Amen.

A Morning Prayer

(by Saint Patrick)

Christ be beside me, Christ be before me,
Christ be behind me, Christ be within me,
Christ be beneath me, Christ be above me,
Christ on my right, Christ on my left,
Christ in my lying down, Christ in my sitting,
Christ in my rising, Light of my life.
Christ be in all hearts thinking about me,
Christ be on all tongues telling of me,
Christ be the vision in eyes that see me,
In ears that hear me, Christ ever be.
Amen.

The Apostle's Creed

I believe in God, the Father almighty,
Creator of heaven and earth,
and in Jesus Christ, his only Son, our Lord,
who was conceived by the Holy Spirit,
born of the Virgin Mary,
suffered under Pontius Pilate,
was crucified, died and was buried;
He descended into hell; on the third day
he rose again from the dead;
He ascended into heaven,
and is seated at the right hand of God
the Father almighty; from there he will
come to judge the living and the dead.
I believe in the Holy Spirit,
the holy catholic Church,
the communion of saints,
the forgiveness of sins,
the resurrection of the body,
and life everlasting. Amen.

Prayer to my Guardian Angel

Angel of God, my guardian dear,
to whom God's love commits me here.
Ever this day be at my side, to light and
guard, to rule and guide. Amen.

When we examine our conscience, we think about some of the ways we can love God and others and some of the ways we can fail to love God and others through sin. The Ten Commandments tell us how we should love and respect God and other people. When we follow them we say yes to God. They are the way to friendship with God.

1 **I am the Lord your God, you shall not have strange gods before Me**

It is good to pray to God and to love Him. It is good to say yes to Him Who loves us. It is good to trust Him Who loves us. We should not put anything (money or the things we own and want to own) before God. God is first in our lives. We should follow God's word and not any horoscopes or fortune tellers.

Q: Do I remember to say my prayers and to trust God?

2 **You shall not take the name of the Lord your God in vain**

It is good to say God's name with respect and to listen to Him in church. It is good to say yes to Him Who leads us.

Q: Do I misbehave in church? Do I use Jesus' name in the wrong way?

3 **Remember to keep holy the Lord's Day**

It is good to go to Mass on Sundays and Holy Days. It is good to say yes to Him Who carries us yet gives us our freedom.

Q: Do I miss Mass on Sundays and Holy Days through my own fault?

4 **Honor your father and your mother**

It is good to love our parents and to be respectful and obedient to them. It is good to say yes to our family.

Q: Am I sometimes disobedient or disrespectful to my parents?

5 **You shall not kill**

It is good to be kind and gentle in our words and actions toward others so that we do not hurt them. It is good to say yes to life.

Q: Am I ever unkind and hurtful to others?
Do I fight and do mean things?
Do I try to forgive those who have hurt me?

6 **You shall not commit adultery**

It is good to be pure in all we say and do.
It is good to love and to respect ourselves and others.
It is good to say yes to pure and responsible love.

Q: Do I think and do bad things to myself or others?
Do I say bad words?

7 **You shall not steal**

It is good to respect others and what belongs to them. We should not cheat.

Q: Have I ever taken something belonging to someone else? Do I share with others who are very poor?
Do I ever cheat?

8 **You shall not bear false witness against your neighbor**

It is good to be honest and not tell lies. We should not speak badly about other people.
It is good to say yes to truth.

Q: Do I always tell the truth, or do I tell lies?
Do I tell mean stories about other people?

9 **You shall not covet your neighbor's wife**

10 **You shall not covet your neighbor's goods**

It is good to be grateful for the things I have and the blessings God has given me. We should not be jealous of other people, of what they own, or of their relationships. It is good to say yes to respect for others and what is theirs.

Q: Am I sometimes greedy and selfish?
Am I sometimes jealous of others?

1 **Altar:** the raised table where the priest stands for the Consecration. The Israelites offered sacrifices of animals to God on altars, now Jesus offers Himself to God for us to wipe away our sins.

2 **Sanctuary:** the entire area at the front of the church where the Mass is celebrated—with the altar, the crucifix, the ambo, the tabernacle, and seating for the priest and servers. We should not run around here!

3 **Stations of the Cross:** images telling the story of Jesus' Way of the Cross. Have a look; there are fourteen.

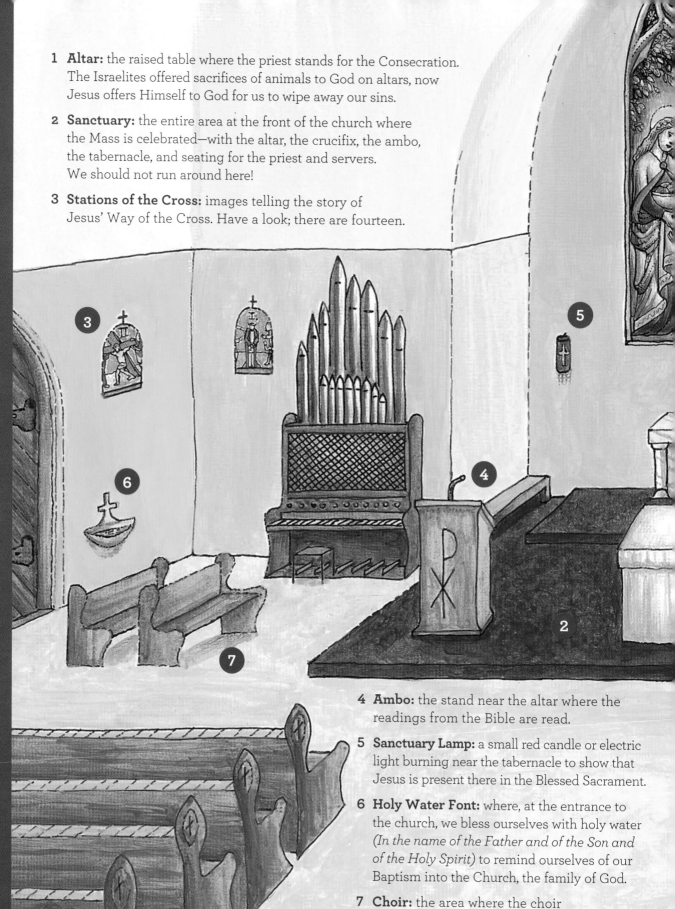

4 **Ambo:** the stand near the altar where the readings from the Bible are read.

5 **Sanctuary Lamp:** a small red candle or electric light burning near the tabernacle to show that Jesus is present there in the Blessed Sacrament.

6 **Holy Water Font:** where, at the entrance to the church, we bless ourselves with holy water (*In the name of the Father and of the Son and of the Holy Spirit*) to remind ourselves of our Baptism into the Church, the family of God.

7 **Choir:** the area where the choir makes music and sings.

11 Sacristy: the room near the sanctuary where the priest and altar servers put on their vestments before Mass.

12 Confessional/Reconciliation Room: the place where we meet Jesus through the priest in Confession.

13 Baptismal Font: a large bowl often made of stone or metal where the people are baptized.

14 Baptistry: the part of the church where Baptisms are performed.

8 Tabernacle: Jesus is present here under the appearance of bread. When we receive Holy Communion we too become tabernacles for Jesus, a lovely home for Him to live in. We genuflect (or bend our right knee to touch the ground) when we pass the tabernacle because Jesus is really present there. This is a way to show Jesus our love and respect. Whenever we visit a church we can sit or kneel in front of Jesus in the tabernacle and talk with Him.

9 The Crucifix: the cross with the image of Jesus.

10 Paschal Candle: an extra-large candle, a symbol of the Risen Christ, used during the Easter season and at the celebration of Baptism.

Explanations

1. In the Jewish tradition of that time, couples were first betrothed before they were married. Betrothal was indeed the first stage of marriage, and the betrothed (the man and woman) made a real and even contractual commitment to marriage. During the betrothal time the couple did not live together.

2. Through the death and Resurrection of Jesus Christ all peoples can receive the gift of new life as children of God and go to heaven. Jesus gave His life freely for this purpose. He established the Church as His Body and His saving Presence in the world since He ascended into heaven. It is His design, His plan, that through the Church the human race comes to eternal life. The Catholic Church therefore is inseparably linked to Christ's work of salvation. She participates in His mission and has, so to say, a partnership role in this task.

   Christ established Himself as the Head of His Body, the Church, of which we as baptized Christians are members. We therefore join in this mission of drawing all peoples to the Father. Ours is the task of proclaiming the good news of the Father's great love for each one of us, of His wondrous gift of new and eternal life through Christ as children of the Father. This message of truth, life and joy is for every person. For those who never hear the gospel message—it is even for them—it is only through Christ and His Church that they can go to heaven. How this happens is known only to God, but we should remember that each day the sacrifice of the Mass is offered not only for Christians but for all men and women of good will (Eucharistic Prayer IV).

   Jesus is *the way and the truth and the life* (John 14:6), and He is the Way to heaven. God's gift of salvation is for all, and through Christ's salvific work and His Church this gift is made available for all. Jesus gives the directive that all peoples and nations should hear this message and through faith in Him and Baptism become members of His family, the Church. It is therefore His gift and our responsibility to share with others the riches He has in store for them. God judges and offers provision for all. It follows that any person who receives entrance to eternal life, including a person who does not know Christ before he dies, enters only through Christ and His Church. This is the mysterious work of God.

3. Mortal sins are serious sins that destroy the life of God, or sanctifying grace, which we received into our souls at Baptism. When we are sorry for our sins and go to a Catholic priest in Confession, these sins are removed and the life of God is restored to our souls. Sins are mortal when three conditions are present:

   (a) It involves a serious matter, e.g., murder, adultery, theft (grave matter is specified by the Ten Commandments).
   (b) The person fully understands and is responsible for what he is doing.
   (c) There is the full consent of the individual or personal choice.

4. Here are the words of absolution said by the priest in Confession:

   God the Father of mercies, through the death and resurrection of His Son, has reconciled the world to Himself and sent the Holy Spirit among us for the forgiveness of sins; through the ministry of the Church may God give you pardon and peace, and I absolve you from your sins in the name of the Father and of the Son and of the Holy Spirit.

5. The *Catechism of the Catholic Church*, an invaluable resource for adults who wish to definitively discover the wealth and wisdom of Catholic teaching, can be referred to for a better appreciation of this mystery. It explains:

   In the most blessed sacrament of the Eucharist the body and blood, together with the soul and divinity, of our Lord Jesus Christ and, therefore, the whole Christ is truly, really, and substantially contained. [202] (ccc 1374)

   202 Council of Trent (1551): DS 1651.

6. This took place approximately in the year 750 A.D. The flesh and blood are still preserved in the town of Lanciano. Scientific research in the laboratories reveal that the flesh is living human heart tissue and the blood is living human blood.

7. The one hour fast required before receiving Holy Communion does not apply to anyone who is sick or anyone who is caring for an ill person.

8. The Pope, the bishops, and the priests receive the Sacrament of Holy Orders. The bishop represents the fullness of this sacrament. He is given the special grace of leading and teaching in the Church, of ordaining priests and other bishops and of celebrating the Sacrament of Confirmation. The Pope is the bishop of Rome, the successor of Peter and the head of the Church on earth. Jesus gave this special call to Peter and to Peter's successors:

   And so I say to you, you are Peter, and upon this rock I will build my Church, and the gates of the netherworld shall not prevail against it. I will give you the keys to the kingdom of heaven: whatever you bind on earth shall be bound in heaven; and whatever you loose on earth shall be loosed in heaven. (Matthew 16:18-19)

9. When the person is close to death, he receives the three sacraments (Confession, Anointing of the Sick, and Eucharist) that give him strength for the last part of the journey through death to his heavenly home in the Father's house.

10. All Christian life and prayer is Trinitarian. When we pray, we pray to the Father through Jesus and by the power of the Holy Spirit. We are baptized in the name of the Trinity, and we live and pray in the Trinity.

My Holy Communion Day

My name:

Date I was born:

My age:

Date of my First Holy Communion:

Name of church:

Name of priest:

Name of school:

My favorite memory of the day:

Names of people who helped me prepare:

Prayer of Thanksgiving

Dear Jesus:

....

....

....

....

....

....

Signed:

....

My First Holy Communion (place photo here)